How to use this book:

Thank you for your purchase; this hand-curated book of Victorian Gothic Haunted Ephemera can be used for: papercraft art, junk journals, scrapbooking, collage, decoupage, card making, mixed media and many other crafts, decorative invitations and gift tags.

Just carefully cut out each image from the book as needed or make photocopies or scans to use them more than once.

I hope you enjoy using the book, the possibilities are limitless. Use the images as a source of inspiration and to boost your creativity.

I hope you have lots of fun making your designs!

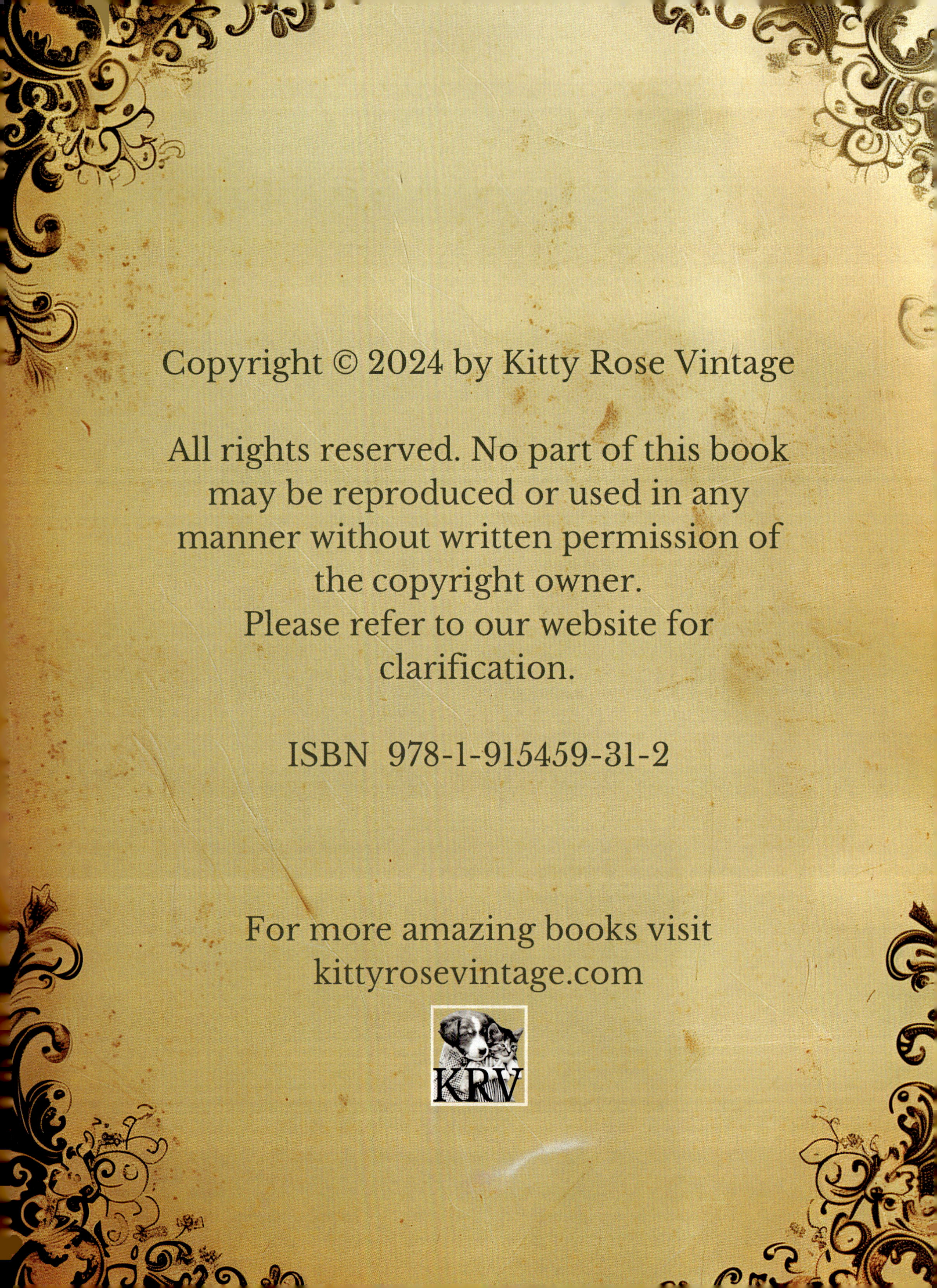

ISBN 978-1-915459-31-2

For more amazing books visit
kittyrosevintage.com